THE LIVING WISDOM OF ANCIENT EGYPT

CHRISTIAN JACQ

THE LIVING WISDOM OF
ANCIENT EGYPT

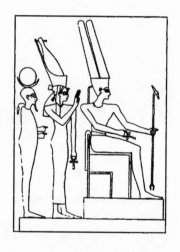

SIMON & SCHUSTER
A VIACOM COMPANY

First published in Great Britain by Simon & Schuster Ltd, 1999
A Viacom Company

1 3 5 7 9 10 8 6 4 2

Simon & Schuster UK Ltd
Africa House
64-78 Kingsway
London WC2B 6AH

Simon & Schuster Australia
Sydney

A CIP catalogue record for this book is available
from the British Library.

ISBN 0-684-85859 2

Typeset by SX Composing DTP, Rayleigh, Essex
Printed and bound in Great Britain by
Bath Press, Bath

For Françoise,
in memory of happy hours spent
in the country of the sages

Contents

Introduction

In the Footsteps of the Sages

Pharaonic Egypt was the country of sages. For more than three thousand years they concerned themselves with the search for spiritual fulfilment through the practice of wisdom which was incarnated in a Goddess, Maat.

Maat is righteousness, right, truth, justness and justice, the immutable law of the universe, coherence and solidarity. She is diametrically opposed to Isefet, chaos, disorder, letting things slide, evil in all its forms.

The Sages of Egypt aimed to open up the spirit and heart with their teachings, making them worthy receptacles for Maat.

Maat is symbolised also as the flight feather of a bird, as the plinth on which rest statues that have been brought to life by rites, and as the rudder which enables Justice to cross the river of existence and land on the banks of eternity.

The term 'Sebayt' or 'Teaching' is formed from the root 'Seba', whose other meanings are 'Door' and 'Star'. Now, these texts really can be seen as doors that open on to the fundamental elements of wisdom and the stars which are destined to guide us on the road of life.

Conquering ignorance is essential. Nobody is born wise and a person has to make serious efforts to develop the qualities needed to be able to 'Speak and achieve Maat' without falling into the twin traps of vanity and greed. Every day the ears, or 'the living', have to be made to listen to words of wisdom; if the teaching is properly understood then righteousness will become a reality. Just acts, conforming to the precepts of Maat, are born out of this understanding. A deed done without egotism is a useful, shining example to others, providing it obeys the golden rule: to act for he who acts.

'The one who knows reality, the myths and the rituals' is how the Egyptian sage portrays himself, a vigilant heart and a plain tongue, capable of satisfying God and the gods because his entire existence rests on knowledge and not on belief. An adept of calm and of silence, he distances himself from the rash, the gossip and the envious. Accomplishing what is right, finding virtue in everything, never evading responsibility, respecting what is worthy, these are just some of the sage's daily duties.

It is because Egyptian civilisation knew how to mould people of this quality that it has conquered time, barbarism, invaders and destructive frenzy. Despite these troubles, this wisdom continues to shine and it can touch our lives. And it is undoubtedly this wisdom that is the true secret of the Ancient Egyptians.

What do we know about the sages, the authors of these teachings? Among them are the Pharaohs like Amenemhet I who wrote a spiritual testament for his successor Sesostris I to share his experiences and to give him guidance on the art of governing with wisdom. Before him another king had done the same for the future Pharaoh Merikare. It is quite probable that many rulers drew up this type of document but their works have been lost. Perhaps they lie there still, sleeping under the sands.

Hor-Djedef, the son of the Pharaoh Cheops, the famous builder of the Great Pyramid at Giza, has left us a 'teaching' which has given him a reputation for wisdom, an indispensable attribute for one of the king's councillors. The viziers who were appointed by Pharaoh to put into practice the virtues of Maat in society, were also the authors of teachings, such as Ptah-Hotep, whose words have been miraculously preserved on a single sheet of papyrus. It was at the age of 110, traditionally attributed to the sages, that this vizier of the sixth dynasty judged it time to put down his experiences on paper to preserve them for future generations. And the first known 'teaching', of which only the beginning has survived, was addressed to Kagemni, the vizier of the Pharaohs Houni and Snefru, the founder of the IVth dynasty. It is likely that Imhotep, the genial builder of the step pyramids at Saqqara, wrote down precepts which are still to be discovered, as is his tomb.

Other sages, like Ipu-Or, are prophets: they predicted the catastrophes which await if the Rule of Maat is not respected. In the chaos and misfortune only one solution will lead us back to harmony: the rediscovery of wisdom.

In the New Empire, the time of the splendour of Karnak and the Valley of the Kings, two figures stand out: Ani, a medium-ranking civil servant who wrote a 'teaching' directed at his spiritual son, and Amenemope, a scribe of Thoth who supervised the land registry and the weights and measures. Like Ptah-Hotep, their works were widely distributed and certain passages of the Book of Proverbs were inspired by Amenemope.

Hardly any anecdotes about the sages exist and we have to wait for the dying embers of Egyptian civilisation and the 'Teaching of Ankh-Sheshonk' to learn that the latter completed his work in prison. The sage had discovered a plot against the King but had not informed anyone because his best friend was involved. But at least we know that he was not just some edifying legend: even in prison the sage thought only of transmitting his teaching.

In this anthology we are not limited to just the 'Teachings', since the *Texts of the Pyramids*, the *Texts of the Sarcophagi*, the *Book of the Dead*, the writings engraved on the walls of the temples and stelae, the stories in the *Tale of the Oases* and other documents provide us with sayings of great diversity. Out of this great wealth of writings we have made a choice favouring those precepts whose authenticity we can, with a high degree of certainty, feel to be established. It is important to realise that these texts are often extremely difficult and that many of these passages still pose insoluble problems. Excavations should not only be limited to monuments; wonderful discoveries lie in store for those researchers who explore the many forms of Egyptian literature.

This book aims to be a guide or a path through the landscape of Egyptian thought and it proves, if proof be needed, that the awesome voice of the Sages of Ancient Egypt still lives on. This voice still speaks to us with astonishing vigour and provides answers to fundamental questions. Surely the question they pose is valid today: what could possibly be more important and more urgent than the quest for wisdom?

1

The Power of the Word of the Sages

The scribes full of wisdom
Since the time which came after the Gods
Whose prophecies came true
Their names will last forever.
They have no longer planned to leave behind them
Anything for their heirs,
The children of their flesh who preserve their name:
They have for an inheritance
Their teachings and the books they have written.
The books they have made their priests,
The tablet of the scribe they have made their beloved
son.
Their teachings are their Pyramids,
The pen was their son,
The writing tablet their bride. . .
The sages predicted the future,
And what they prophesied came true.
When one discovers something to be a proverb
It is found in their writings.
Although they have disappeared,
Their magical power touches all those who read their
writings

Text: A.H. Gardiner, *Hieratic Papyri in the British Museum*

Let us begin with the commands for learning about life,
These are the instructions for well-being;
All the rules for relationships with the Ancient Ones,
For conduct towards dignitaries,
To know how to reply to those who talk to you,
To respond to those who send a message,
To guide those who listen on the Roads of Life
And make them prosper on Earth,
To make his heart enter into the temple
While avoiding evil.

Amenemope

Harken: I have given you excellent advice,
Keep it in your heart,
Act accordingly,
You will become a complete being,
All evil will avoid you.

Ani

Read these texts well:
They inform and they educate.
They make the fool wise.
If you read them to an ignorant man,
He will be enlightened thanks to them.
Fill yourself with these texts,
Keep them in your heart.

Amenemope

2

The Path of Righteousness

Living in accordance with Maat, Goddess of Justice

Righteousness (Maat) appears in the heart of the Divine Light.

Temple of Ibis at Khargah Oasis

Truth is sent by God.

Ani

Truth is a great gift from God.
He grants it to those He wants.
The power of those who try to be like Him is such that it saves the unfortunate from persecution.

Amenemope

Do justice (Maat) for the master of justice (Maat) whose justness is truly just.

Stories of the Oases

You who enter the temple of Ptah and leave. . .
You shall love life,
You shall forget death.
I have put justice (Maat) in her place,
In the knowledge that this was God's desire.

Statue of Tja-ba-neb Dedenimou

Were I able to see the truth before the Master of all.
Were I able to offer righteousness to the Lord of the Universe.
I shall live alongside the master of my life,
I shall act according to his commands.

Texts of the Sarcophagi, Ch.534

Establish the place of Maat for the Pharaoh,
Since righteousness is what Pharaoh loves.
Say to Pharaoh that this is what the nature of Maat is,
Since it is truth that the King loves.

Kagemni

Pharaoh has put righteousness (Maat) in the place of wickedness.

Texts of the Pyramids, 1775b

Righteousness is fitting for a Pharaoh.
It is the interior of the household that makes you respect the exterior.

Merikare

I have glorified the Law (Maat) which embraces the
Divine Principle,
I know that it exists there.
Maat is also my bread,
I drink her dew,
With her I form a complete being.

Sayings of the Pharaoh Queen Hatshepsut

The light of Heaven is placed in harmony for Pharaoh.
For Pharaoh it reconciles duality into harmony.
For Pharaoh the darkness is placed in harmony.
Universal harmony is what is brought before Pharaoh,
It is what he sees and hears.
Universal harmony surrounds Pharaoh,
Universal harmony belongs to him.

Texts of the Pyramids, 34

The balanced happiness of a country is the result of the
accomplishment of justice.

Stories of the Oases

The strength of a Pharaoh lies in justice.
A destroyer's monuments are themselves destroyed.
The acts of a liar do not last.

Kanais, Inscription of Seti I

Great is the Law (Maat),
Its efficiency lasting.
The Law has not been disturbed since the time of Osiris.
When the end comes,
The Law will remain.

Ptah-Hotep

It has been so designed that Truth (Maat) comes to the
sage in accordance with the words of the ancients.

Merikare

A great man lives with righteousness (Maat).
Evil (Isefet) is what he hates.
He is counted among the venerable ones,
He is the companion of right.

Brooklyn Papyrus

All through your earthly life,
Accomplish righteousness.
Comfort those who suffer,
Do not oppress the widow,
Do not drive a man from the land of his father,
Do not hinder the great from fulfilling their duties,
Do not punish people unjustly.

Merikare

All my life was spent in public service.

The seal of office that I received I kept to the end of my life.

It was never far from me even when I rested.

When words were said against me in front of judges I was innocent and the false accusations rebounded on the heads of my accusers.

Every act I did, I did effectively, because I was a virtuous servant.

Meir, inscription of Pepi-Ankh

I have practised and preached the justice of Maat,

I have told the truth,

I have spoken just words.

I have acted with justice,

To profit by the love of mankind.

I have dealt justly with those who challenge it.

I have saved the weak from the clutches of the strong as much as I could.

I have given bread to those who were hungry,

Water to those who were thirsty,

Clothes to those who have none.

I have allowed those without a boat

To cross to the other bank.

I have given an eternal dwelling place

To those who have no sons to build them one.

Mastaba of Sheshi at Saqqara

I have done justice for its Master,
I have satisfied God with the things He loves.
I have spoken and repeated words of righteousness.
I have codified righteousness and delivered justice.
I have given bread to the hungry,
Clothes to the naked,
I have respected my father,
I have profited from the love of my mother and achieved
self mastery.
I have never slandered anyone,
Because I wanted the accomplishment and the respect of
Gods and men for ever.

Mastaba of Idu at Saqqara

See to those things that can be justly accomplished.
Do justice to every man.
A judge has to have a visible face.
The water and the wind bear witness to his deeds which
none can be unaware of.

Tomb of Rekhmir at Thebes.
Lines on the installing of a Vizier

Do not automatically take the side of a well-dressed man,
Do not automatically turn away from the badly dressed
man.
Do not accept gifts from powerful men,
Do not be unjust towards the weak man to help the
strong.

Amenemope

All conduct should be so straight that you can measure it
with a plumb-line.

Ptah-Hotep

Keep closely to the Law,
Never overstep it.

Ptah-Hotep

Maat and Eternal Life

Be aware of eternity appproaching,
The vital thing is to practise justice.

Stories of the Oases

He who is without righteousness will not enter the
dwelling of Maat, the country of silence.
Only those whose hearts are true are admitted on to the
ferry,
Since the ferryman will not take the unrighteous.
How fortunate they are, those who pass to the other side!

Hymn to Amon

Unjust acts do not come home to port.
The just man will always reach port.

Stories of the Oases

Glory be to you, Harmony of the Universe, sovereign of the north wind!
You breathe life into the living,
You constantly give a wind to those who sail in your ship. . .
Allow me to enter the fields of Paradise, to reach the place of offerings and be nourished forever on all the sacrificial tables of the city of the pillar.
How my heart moves in the realm of the underworld.
May the road of Heaven be open for me.

Stele at the British Museum

I was a man both correct and just,
Free from disloyalty,
Who kept God in his heart,
Having been instructed in his power.
I reached this city of Eternity
After acting well on earth.
I never caused affliction,
No reproach was ever laid against me.
My name was never said negatively
In connection with any vice.
I knew the joy of following righteousness,
Since I knew that it was filled with light
For those who do good on the earth,
From birth to death.
It is a solid defence for those who testify,
On that day when they appear before the heavenly court,
Which judges the unfortunate,
Strips them naked,
Punishes the guilty and destroys their souls.
I have led a virtuous life.
Listen to me, you who walk on this earth:
Practise righteousness each day,
It is a food that can't be eaten enough.

You will transcend your existence with happiness of heart
Until that moment when your spirit passes to the beautiful West.
Your soul will have the power to come and go,
Like the Masters of eternity
Who have vanished with their ancestors.

Stele at Beki

Make beautiful your resting place in the West,
Make splendid your resting place in the City of the Dead.
Thanks to your correctness and just way of life
It is there that your heart and soul can rest.

Merikare

Righteousness is eternal.
It descends into the Underworld with those who practise it.
It is placed in the tomb,
It is united with the earth,
But its name never fades,
What it has achieved is remembered.
Such is the Law and the Divine command.

Stories of the Oases

If you lead a righteous life,
You will become young again in your time.
You will shed your years like a frog its skin,
You will return as you are now.

The song of the harpist Nefer-Sekhou

Good and Evil

Learn to understand the words which distinguish good from evil.

Amon-Nakht

Do not respond with evil to good.
Do not confuse the one thing with the other.

Stories of the Oases

It is to those who do evil that evil, inevitably, will be done.

Urkenden VI

The heart of God is full of sadness because of the evil that He has to punish.
If retribution does not come sooner it comes later.

A law at the temple of Edfou

I have spent my days searching for good,
I have peacefully become a respected man,
I have upheld righteousness in accordance to your
Majesty,
Day after day.
I have been a fair and just man,
Free from evil,
My heart has never joined with wickedness.
I was a just man,
Never giving in to favouritism,
Someone whose bearing was measured,
Whose words made good sense,
A respected man who followed the paths of God,
And who was free from injustice.
If you do good,
Good will be done unto you.
It will benefit you in the long run,
In accordance with what you will have achieved.

Statue of Ankh-pa-Khered in Cairo Museum

I have come having chased away the evil that was in my
heart
And controlled the disorder that was in me.
I have come to bring righteousness,
Which has appeared in the form of this creative power
Which nourishes humanity and comes from God.

Texts of the Sarcophagi, Ch.306

Even if he were an important person, a man whose nature
is evil does not know how to remain upright.

Ani

31

You cannot remove the venom from the crocodile, from the serpent and from the evil man.

Ankh-Sheshonk

Even the smallest serpent is venomous.

Ankh-Sheshonk

When you get to see the whole length of a crocodile, you can appreciate the fear that the sight provokes.
A crocodile does not die from great distress, he dies from hunger.

Ankh-Sheshonk

Injustice exists in abundance,
But evil can never succeed in the long run.

Ptah-Hotep

It is the duty of responsible men to fight evil and affirm goodness,
As they are the workmen who bring into existence that which has to be.

Stories of the Oases

Punish with principle,
Teach meaningfully.
The act of stopping evil leads to the lasting establishment of virtue.

Ptah-Hotep

It only takes a moment to put something right,
But evil lasts a long time.

Stories of the Oases

Even a little evil rushes towards death,
Even a little good act is not hidden from God.

Ankh-Sheshonk

3

The God of the Sages

God is One

You are the One.
No father conceived you,
No mother gave birth to you.

Hymn to Ptah

You are unique,
You are He who existed before existence,
You are the Creator of Heaven and Earth,
Who offers plenty to all without cease.

Lyons Stele 88

The One who is unique created all that exists,
And the Earth appeared for the first time.
His origins are mysterious,
His forms innumerable,
His beginning is unknown. . .
All living things came into existence when He was born.
Nothing exists beyond Him.
He hides Himself in His true manifestation,
A shining lamp, full of light.

Cairo Papyrus 58032

God is the Sculptor who sculpted His own form,
The Modeller who has never been modelled,
The Unique One who travels eternity.

Hymn of the architects Souti and Hor

He is the One who created himself and whose form
remains unknown,
A perfect creation who reveals Himself in sacred sym-
bols,
Who created Himself and His statues,
A great power who acted according to His heart,
Whose seed fertilised His body,
And whose womb gave birth in the Heart of Mystery.

Hymn to Amon at Leyde

One who remains unique,
Creating beings,
One who remains unique,
Possessor of numberless arms.
A unique Form who created all that exists,
One who created all living things and remains One,
From His eyes came Man,
From His mouth the Gods were born.

Hymn to Amon at Cairo

Multiple Gods

There are three Gods: Amon, Ra and Ptah.
As Amon His Name is hidden,
His face is the divine light, Ra,
His body, Ptah.

Hymn to Amon at Leyde

The Eight were Your first Manifestation,
Until You had perfected Your number,
Being the One.
Your body is hidden amongst the Ancient Ones,
You hide Yourself as Amon at the head of the Gods.

Hymn to Amon at Leyde

God reveals Himself in millions of forms.

Ani

The Hidden God

Amongst mankind, generation succeeds generation.
God, who knows their hearts, is hidden.

Ani

The hiding place which veils the Gods is unique,
And does not reveal its true form.
None of them knows its true nature, which is not
revealed in any writing.
No one can describe it,
It is too vast to be understood,
Too mysterious to be known.
If anyone pronounces its secret name they will be
destroyed.

Hymn to Amon at Leyde

You are Amon, the Hidden God,
Lord of Silence,
Who comes when the humble call,
You give life to those without it.

Stele at Berlin

God appears unseen on the wind.
His presence fills the night.
He creates what is above in Heaven as He does what is
below on the Earth.

Tablet from Cairo

God is found in the primordial waters,
They do not make him unknowable,
That which is hidden there manifests itself.

Merikare

Those who say: 'That can't happen' should take a look at
what is hidden.
Every day God reveals the secrets of His creation on the
Earth.

Ankh-Sheshonk

God and Man

Man is clay and straw,
God is the builder,
Each day He demolishes and builds.

Amenemope

The human race never accomplishes anything.
It's what God commands that gets done.

Ptah-Hotep

God is always perfect.
Man is always imperfect.
The words of men are one thing,
The actions of God another.

Amenemope

If destiny and fortune exist,
It is because God has sent them.

Insinger Papyrus

The Paths of God

Oh my twice-great master Thoth,
The Only One,
Who has no equal,
Who sees and hears whoever passes.
Who knows whoever comes,
With the knowledge of everything that happens!
You have made my heart walk upon your waters,
He who walks on your road will never stumble.

Petosiris

Oh people living on this Earth,
And those yet to be born,
You who come to this mountain,
You will see this tomb and pass by it.
Come, I will guide you on the Road of Life,
You will sail with a favourable wind, without accidents,
And you will arrive at the abode of the City of
Generations.
The road of the man who obeys God is straight.
Happy is he whose heart urges him to follow it!

Petosiris

To walk on the road of God is to be filled with light,
Great are the advantages gained by those who
Discipline themselves to follow it.
It is a monument raised by them on this Earth,
Those who follow the Paths of God,
Those who cling to the Ways of God,
Spend all their lives in joy,
Gathering riches without equal.

Petosiris

Those whom God guides do not go wrong.
Those whose boat He takes away cannot cross.

Ptah-Hotep

Serving God

Celebrate the monthly ceremony of the Servant of God,
Put on your sacred sandals,
Go to the temple,
Enter the Sanctuary,
Eat the bread of the Temple of God,
Renew the libations on the altar,
Add to the offerings,
Take good care of your monuments as a duty of your
power.
A single day can be the equivalent of Eternity,
A single hour can suffice for the future,
Since God knows who acts for Him.

Merikare

Celebrate the feast of your God,
And begin it at the correct time.
God is unhappy if He is neglected.

Ani

Venerate God on your road,
Whatever form He may take,
Whether it be of precious stones or embodied in a copper
statue.
One form will replace another form,
As the annual floods follow the annual floods.

Merikare

All that can be surveyed, from the beginning to the end
of the measuring cord, is His domain.
His royal rule measures the stones,
He places the measuring cord on the Earth,
He gives justice to the countries and temples.
Every city is under His shadow,
His heart moves according to His will.
Hymns are sung to Him in the temples,
Every place of work exists thanks to His love.
On festival days beer is brewed for Him,
The night is spent awake reflecting on His miracles,
While His name is chanted from the roof of the Temple
And His song rises to Heaven.

Hymn to Amon at Leyde

My heart inclines to You,
Master of the Constellations.
Thanks to You my hunger is satisfied without food,
My thirst is quenched without drinking. . .
You are a father to the motherless,
A husband for the widow.
How sweet it is to say Your name!
It tastes of life,
The taste of bread for a child.
He clothes the naked,
He is like food for the spirit.

Graffito on the tomb of Pairi

May no part of me be without God.
May Thoth the God of Knowledge protect me.

The Second Book of Breath

Mingle with the Gods in Heaven,
May no one be able to distinguish between you and one
of Them.
May your body become like His which both exists, yet
does not exist, for all eternity.

Ritual of the Opening of the Mouth

God and Light

God created the light and the darkness in which all
creation exists.

Ankh-Sheshonk

You are the Divine Light who has appeared in Heaven
And lights up the Earth with the perfection of Your shining eye,
You who came from the Ocean of Beginning,
Who appeared from the primordial waters,
Who created everything,
Who formed the Great Union of the Gods,
Who is self-begotten in His chosen forms.

Amenhotep, son of Hapu

You appear in perfection on the horizon of Heaven,
A living Disc, the origin of Life!
From the moment that You rise in the eastern skies
You fill all beauty with Your beauty;
You are abundance, You are great and shining, rising
above the land.

The Great Hymn to Aton

You call on the Divine Light,
It is the Master of Forms who listens,
It is the Master Creator who replies.

Song of the Harpist

When I walk upon the celestial waters,
I worship the sunrise like the light of my own eye.
I am the Great God, I have come into existence.
I gather my names.
Yesterday belongs to me, I know tomorrow.
I am the phoenix, there is no impurity in me.
I know the way,
I aim for the isles of the just,
I reach the country of light,
I restore my sight,
I see the light,
I am one of the beings of light who lives in the light.

The Book of Leaving the Day, Ch.64

I am the divine Light, master of the light.
The Word is mine.
It is thanks to the Word I can cross the sky.

Texts of the Sarcophagi, Ch.818

I am the hidden form at the centre of the light.
I go through fire and emerge without harm.

Texts of the Sarcophagi, Ch.246

Pharaoh has placed a divine light for him which is like a
heavenly stair beneath his feet.

Texts of the Pyramids, 11808

You have the light in your hands,
You will appear by day like the perfect glow of the
divine light spreading over the whole world.

Embalming Ritual

Divine light,
Allow me to be one of your companions,
A member of the crew that sails in your heavenly ship.

Florence Stele

4

The Sage and the Universe

Celestial Energy

O you who dwell in the ocean of energy,
Near Heaven,
Prepare a ship for me that I might sail to the realm of
light.

Texts of the Sarcophagi, Ch.815

I follow the Great God,
Who has created Himself.
Who is He?
Energy.
The ocean of primordial energy,
The father of the Gods.

Tomb of Queen Nefertari

I am the South,
I am the North,
I am the East,
I am the West,
I am the master of the universe.
I emerged from the ocean of primordial energy at the
same time as the divine light.

The Second Book of Breaths

I am a follower of the divine light,
I have taken possession of Heaven.
I have come to You, my father Ra, divine light.
I have travelled light-filled space,
I have called upon the Great One,
I have travelled through the Word,
I have crossed into the solitude of the shadows which lie
on the road to the divine light.
I have gained Heaven.

The Book of Leaving the Day, Ch.131

Three is for Heaven,
Two is for the Earth.

Texts of the Pyramids, 2156c

The Stars

I shall ascend into the space of light,
I shall cross the face of the Earth,
I shall walk in the light
And I shall wait upon the stars.

Texts of the Sarcophagi, Ch.545

Can you rise,
Can you reach up to Heaven like a great star rising in the
East.

Texts of the Pyramids, 1038

You can be sure that this star has been placed above the
world in the West, and you shall never perish.

Texts of the Sarcophagi Ch.9

The face of the reborn is uncovered.
He sees the master of the realm of light while he travels
the sky,
He appears like a great God,
Master of eternity,
Undying star.

Texts of the Sarcophagi, Ch .88

I rejoiced since I have touched Heaven.
My head has pierced the sky.
I have felt the very stars,
I have reached joy,
So that I shine like a star,
And dance like the great constellations.

Tomb of Sarenput at Aswan

I have flown like the swallow,
I have soared like the falcon.
I have risen to the place where Justice lies,
I have flown to the Blessed like the swallow.
The swallows are the undying stars who give the Pharaoh
The Tree of Life in which they live.

Texts of the Pyramids, 1770a
Texts of the Sarcophagi, Ch.205

Nature

The primordial whole of the Two Lands in union,
Nourishment and substance before the Ennead, the Union of the Gods,
A shining spirit among shining spirits:
It is for his sake that the waters of the ocean of primordial energy move.
It is for his sake that the north wind blows south,
It is so he can breathe that Heaven gives us air
And his heart knows contentment.
Plants grow thanks to his heart,
And the shining Earth gives forth abundance.
The sky above and the stars obey him.

Stele at the Louvre C 286

The sight of men clears when they see You.
The trees turn toward His face,
Towards His single eye,
And their leaves open.
The fish leap in the sea,
The cattle gambol,
The birds flap their wings,
They perceive Him in His moment of perfection.
If they have life, it is because they see Him every day.

Hymn to Amon at Leyde

The Word is found in the ox,
Intuition in the cows.
Let them be fed without delay.

Petosiris

Pharaoh lives on the sweet fruits of the tree and the perfumes of the Earth.

Texts of the Pyramids, 718c

Fill your arms with as many flowers as you can see.
All are needed, for it is good not to be deprived of them.

Ani

There is no river in existence that allows itself to be hidden, for it will destroy the dam that conceals it.

Merikare

5

Time and the Sage

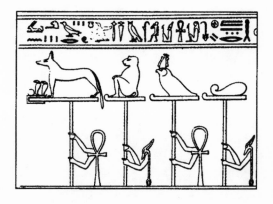

Righteousness has existed since the time of our ancestors, justice came down from Heaven and united those on Earth. It was a time of plenty, the winds were mild and in the Two Lands famine was unknown. In the days of the ancient gods the walls did not crumble and fall and the thorn did not prick.

Urkunden VIII, 90

Neither worry about, nor rejoice in, the future.

Stories of the Oases

Do not prepare today for tomorrow before it is there.
In the eyes of God isn't yesterday the same as today?

Černy and Gardiner, Hieratic Ostraca

Yesterday belongs to me and I know the future.

Texts of the Sarcophagi, Ch.335

This world will return to the primordial ocean, to the infinity that was its original state. The main creator will dwell with Osiris after taking the form of another serpent that men will not know and the Gods do not see.

The Book of Leaving the Day, Ch.175

I am the Eternal One,
I am the divine light which came out of the primordial energy in my role as Creator.
Ba, my spirit, is divine.
I am He who created the Word.
I am reborn each day,
My life is eternity.

Texts of the Sarcophagi, Ch.307

A single day can last eternity.

Merikare

The male eternity and the female eternity are the sum of existence. The first is the day, the second the night.

Texts of the Sarcophagi, Ch.335

May my reward be a wonderful place in Heaven, so that I may spring out of the Earth as a spirit bird to look upon the Master of the Gods.

Chester Beatty IV Papyrus

O you living beings on the Earth who pass before my
tomb,
Whether you travel upstream or down,
Say these words:
May offerings of thousands of loaves and pitchers of
beer be made to he
Who dwells here.
Thus I shall live eternally in the sacred earth.

Tomb of Hirkhuf at Aswan

There is no place for the rebel in Heaven.

Stele at Cairo 20538

6

The Science of the Sage

The Heart

The Ennead, the Union of the Gods, created sight for the eyes, sound for the ears and breath for the nose.

These organs carry perception straight to the heart. It is thanks to the heart that all knowledge exists, language formulates what the heart understands. In this way all creative powers come into existence, being and non-being (Atum) and his Ennead.

Every divine word reveals itself in the secret thoughts of the heart and the way that we speak. In this way too, creative energies and the qualities of being come into existence. All food and sustenance were created thanks to the Word.

In this way life has been granted to the just and death to the unjust.

Thus were created all work and trades, the action of the hands and the movement of the legs, the mobility of every limb and joint, conforming as the heart understands and language gives order which continually creates the meaning of everything.

A tablet at Shabaka

You are the shepherd Amon, you lead the flock to fresh pastures.
Can you lead me to nourishment, you the tireless shepherd.
A light will shine in whoever places you in his heart.

Ostracon British Museum 565 a

The initiate is a being whose secrets of the heart are revealed, pure in thought and deed when he performs the sacred rites.

Griffith Studies p. 287

The heart of Man is a gift from God.
Take care not to neglect it.

Amenemope

Your life runs true when heart and words are without fault.

Ankh-Sheshonk

Follow your heart all your life,
Do not commit excess with respect to what has been ordained.
Do not cut short the time for following your heart.
To waste a single moment of actions of the heart is an insult to the Ka, your soul.
Do not divert your daily routine excessively to support your household.
When things happen, follow your heart.
The negligent will never profit.

Ptah-Hotep

Follow your heart all the length of your days and make each day perfect.

Stele at the British Museum 37984

Never separate your heart from your words. Then you will succeed in life.

Amenemope

Hold fast to your heart.
Strengthen your heart.
Do not try to guide a ship with just your tongue.
If language is the rudder of a ship,
Then the Master of Totality has to be the pilot.

Amenemope

My heart has encouraged me to do my duty with my conduct.
It is, for me, a perfect witness.
I do not break its rules,
I am afraid to ignore its commandments.
If I have known great prosperity,
It is thanks to His influence on my actions.
I have followed His teachings to the letter.
A divine word is like a heart beating in every body.

Urkunden IV 974

Take heed of my words,
Be competent in every task.
Make your heart a solid wall against which the waves will break.

Amon-Nakht

The character of a righteous man is more agreeable to God than the sacrifice of a dozen oxen from an evil man.

Merikare

Heart of my mother, heart of my being, do not speak against me, do not prosecute me before the Heavenly Court; you are the creative power in my body, the creator who gives life to my limbs.

The Book of Leaving the Day, Ch.30

Knowledge

Let us come and give thanks to Thoth, the God of Knowledge, the measure which embodies correctness in the scales of justice.
He rejects evil and welcomes the man who turns aside from unjust actions.
He is the judge who weighs the words of men,
Who calms the storm,
Who gives peace,
The official scribe who preserves the hidden texts,
He punishes the criminal,
He welcomes the obedient man,
His arm is strong,
The sage at the heart of the Ennead, the Union of Gods,
He who restores what was forgotten,
He who advises the lost,
He who preserves the moment,
He who watches over the hours of night,
He whose words last for eternity.

Statue of Horemheb (Metropolitan Museum of New York)

My ferry allows me to cross to the other side.
Thoth, the God of Knowledge will pilot me as he did the
Eye of Horus.

Texts of the Sarcophagi, Ch.182

I know what is known intuitively,
That which is revealed to the most powerful seers.
May my path be open,
Since I am the master of the Breath of Life.

Texts of the Sarcophagi, Ch.236

Every being who is fully aware does not die a second
death. His enemies can exert no influence over him and
no magic can hinder him on this earth.

Texts of the Sarcophagi, Ch.83

Each man who learns this formula will be a light in the
sky and recognised as having risen from the dead in the
matrix of the stars.
He will descend into the circle of fire.
The flames will never harm him.
His life-span will be happy.

Texts of the Sarcophagi, Ch.1130

Those who know that will be transformed into a son of the Divine Light.
Those who know that will not perish on this earth,
They will experience Eternity.
They will eat bread in the house of Osiris,
They will enter the temple of the Almighty God,
They will receive offerings.

Texts of the Sarcophagi, Ch.1035

The paths to rebirth (Osiris) are in the Heavens.
Those who know the way to cross them are themselves Gods,
They are found in the retinue of the God of Knowledge.
They can travel wherever they wish in Heaven.
Those who do not know how to reach the Sacred Paths will be excluded from the offerings.

Texts of the Sarcophagi, Ch.1035

Those who know find grace.
The ignorant damn themselves.

Law of the temple at Edfou

Magic

God has given magic to man to deflect the blinding effects of what happens.

Merikare

Those who know the Book of Magic can go out by day
and walk the earth with the living.
They will never die.
That has been proven countless times.

The Book of Leaving the Day, Ch.68

Let your thoughts be great magical incantations spoken
by you.

The Book of Leaving the Day, Ch.80

I have come armed with magical spells.
Thus can I quench my thirst,
Since I am master of the Words of Creation.

Texts of the Sarcophagi, Ch.644

So long as I have magical powers I am a being of Light.
I pass by hostile spirits.
They cannot speak to me for fear of Him whose name is
hidden.
He is in me, I know and obey Him.

Texts of the Sarcophagi, Ch.1130

I know the secret of the divine words and the conduct of
Rituals.
I have practised every magic without any of its laws
escaping me.
Nothing has kept its secrets from me.
I see the Divine Light in all its manifestations.

Stele in the Louvre

Seeing

Everything that happens in each country is reported back
to you.
Even when you are in your palace.
You hear the talk from every country,
Your ears are everywhere.
Your eye is brighter than the stars in the skies,
Your vision is clearer than that of the sun.
You hear everything which is said, even if spoken in the
depths of a cave.
Your eye sees everything which is hidden.

Anastasi Papyrus IV, 6

The eye of Pharaoh is his strength.

Texts of the Pyramids, 320b

Pharaoh rises to Heaven like the eye of the Divine Light.
Pharaoh comes and goes in the field of offerings,
Since Pharaoh himself is the eye of the Divine Light.

Texts of the Pyramids, 1231b & 698c-d

I had integrity and was just,
I hated lies and fought each day for truth.
I was a wise man without equals,
A man who shrugged off all difficulties,
I have ordered everything according to the Divine eye.

Stele of Ra-Hotep, High Priest of Ptah

The parts of my body have been put back together,
What was taken away has been brought back,
What was dispersed has been gathered,
My eyes have been opened and I see the Great Star.

Texts of the Sarcophagi, Ch.106

The man who rises from the dead is like the falcon with
his piercing eye, crossing the evening sky.

Texts of the Pyramids, 1048d

I am the Eye of Horus, shining in the night, who creates
fire from his own light.

Texts of the Sarcophagi, Ch.1053

Your eyes are the Ship of the Morning and the Ship of
the Evening.
Your right eye is the Ship of the Evening,
Your left eye is the Ship of the Morning.

Texts of the Sarcophagi, Ch.531

Silence

The commotion in the temple is like a tree growing in an enclosed place.

The growth of its branches lasts but a brief moment, and it finishes as firewood.

It is taken far from its proper place and the fire is its shroud.

The true silent man, who keeps to himself, is like a tree grown in a field.

He matures, increases his production and straightens himself before his master.

The fruits of this tree are sweet, its shadow delicious.

He lives his life peacefully in his garden.

Amenemope

If you work hard,
And if growth takes place as it should in the fields,
It is because God has placed abundance in your hands,
Do not gossip in your neighbourhood,
Because people respect the silent.

Ptah-Hotep

Thoth, place me in Heliopolis, the city of the Eight Gods,
Your town where it is wonderful to dwell.
Give me bread and give me beer,
Keep idle words from my mouth.
May Thoth protect me from the future!
I shall appear in court before the masters of righteous-
ness, I leave speaking justly
The Doum palm is more than sixty cubits high and bears
fleshy fruit full of juicy seeds.
You who gather water to bring it to the lonely places, let
me drink deep since I am a silent man.
Thoth is a well of sweet water for the man thirsting in the
desert.
The well remains sealed to the talkative,
It opens for the silent,
The silent man comes and finds the well,
The disorderly are lost.

Papyrus Sallier 1, 8, 2-6

Happy is he who rests on the arm of Amon which pro-
tects the silent and frees the humble, which gives life to
those who love Him and is a guarantee of a happy old age
in the west of Thebes.

Stele in Berlin 6910

The ship of fools gets stuck in the mud.
The ship of the silent sails with the wind.

Amenemope

It is painful to remain silent while you listen.
But there is no point in replying to the ignorant.
Responding to their proposals creates disorder.
Their hearts will not accept the truth.

Kha-Keper-Re-Seneb

Listening and Understanding

If he who listens, listens fully,
Then he who listens becomes he who understands.
When hearing is good, speech is good.
He who listens becomes the master of what is profitable.
Listening benefits the listener.
To listen is better than anything,
Thus is born perfect love.
God loves he who listens.
He hates those who do not listen.
It is the heart who gives birth to its master,
As he who understands or does not understand.
For a man his heart is life, prosperity and health.
He who listens understands what is said,
He who loves to understand does what is said.

Ptah-Hotep

As for the ignorant man who does not listen,
He accomplishes nothing.
He equates knowledge with ignorance,
The useless with the harmful.
He does everything which is detestable,
So people get angry with him each day.
He lives with that which brings death,
His food is twisted words.
His character is readily recognised by the nobles,
When this is known, life is a living death every day.

Ptah-Hotep

Open your ears,
Listen to these words,
Let your soul understand them.
May you keep them in your heart.
Woe to he who neglects them!
May they stay in your heart of hearts,
May they be locked up in your soul.
If you lead your life with these words in your heart you
will succeed.

Amenemope

Speech

It is not me who speaks,
It is not me who thinks,
It is God who speaks and it is surely He who thinks.

Papyrus of Magic in Brooklyn

The initiate is he who transmits the word of one God to another God.

Texts of the Sarcophagi, VII

The language of Pharaoh is the pilot appointed by Maat. He uses just words.

Texts of the Pyramids, 1776

This is the Word which is found in the shadows.
Inasmuch as every living spirit knows it, they will dwell among the living.

Texts of the Sarcophagi, VII

The Word is with me. Thanks to it I have crossed Heaven.

Texts of the Sarcophagi, VII

Sit yourself down under the leaves of the sycamore trees of the Goddess Hathor, when She travels to the city of the pillar, the bearer of sacred words.

Texts of the Sarcophagi, Ch.225

A perfect word is hidden more deeply than precious stones.
It is to be found near the servants working at the millstone.

Ptah-Hotep

To have strength, be a craftsman with words.
The power of a man lies in his language and words are
more effective than any other form of fighting.

Merikare

Only speak when you have something worth saying.
He who speaks in counsel has to be an excellent crafts-
man with words.
Speaking is more difficult than any other work.

Ptah-Hotep

God hates liars.

Amenemope

Be careful to avoid the mistake of lying: it will prevent
you from fighting the evil inside yourself.

Ani

The body of a man is bigger than all the granaries of
Pharaoh.
He is full of varied responses: choose what is good to say
and keep evil words prisoner in your body.

Ani

Prayer

Do not raise your voice in the temple of God since He
hates loud begging.
Keep a loving heart whose words stay hidden.
He will provide for your needs,
He will listen to what you say,
Your offering will be acceptable to Him.

Ani

Do not ask God for advice and then disregard it.

Ankh-Sheshonk

Language

If the language of man is the rudder of a ship,
Then it is the Master of the whole who is the pilot.

Amenemope

The language of men is their scales.
It is these scales that allow them to measure the weight
of something.

Stories of the Oases

A man can be destroyed because of his language.

Ani

The evil tongue of the stupid man is the sword that will end his life.

Insinger Papyrus

Testimony

Let the one strengthen the other,
Let him work for his predecessor
With the hope that his successor will work on what he will have accomplished.

Merikare

I bring the praise of Amon to the heights of heaven and all over the world.
I evoke his power for he who travels downstream and upstream on the great river.
Watch over His presence,
Bear witness to it to your sons and daughters, to the great and the small.
Speak of Him to the generations in your time as well as to those yet to come.
Speak of it to the fish in the river and the birds in the sky,
To those who know and to those who do not know.

Stele in Berlin 23.077

Teaching

Do not teach those who do not want to hear.

Ankh-Sheshonk

Speak to your children,
Since the Word has been a teaching since the time of God.

The Loyalist Teaching

The twisted stick is thrown to the ground where both light and shade fall on it. But the carpenter can carry it away, straighten it out and fashion a staff for a great noble out of it.

Ani

7

The Behaviour and the Actions of the Sage

As for you, teach your disciple the words of tradition.
May he act as a model for the children of the great,
That they may find in him the understanding and justice
of every heart that speaks to him,
Since man is not born wise.

Ptah-Hotep

I have seen the transformation of the divine principle of
the two regions of light on the secret roads of heaven.
The divine light itself speaks through me. I was bathed in
its radiance and fully nourished by divine wisdom.

Inscription of Tuthmosis III at Karnak

The Sage himself is a teaching for the great.

Merikare

Everyone can master his own nature if the wisdom which
he has been taught has made that nature stable.

Ani

I am silent in the face of anger,
A patient man with the ignorant,
Liking to calm quarrels.
I am tranquil, free from impulses,
Who knows what is ordained to happen and awaits it
serenely.
I am the one who shows himself in conflicts,
And who knows (the better to avoid them) the words
which provoke anger.
I am master of myself,
I am kind and friendly,
I calm those who weep with words of comfort.
I have a kindly face for those who call on me,
I help my fellow man.
I can see through deceit when it occurs,
My face is radiant, my hand is far reaching,
And I do not hold back for myself the food that I have.
I am the one who is known for that which is not known,
The one who teaches what is useful.
I am someone who listens and acts with integrity,
And meditates on correctness in my heart.
I am someone who carries out his duty,
Who stays calm, free from overexcitement,
I accomplish deeds without haste,
I am reliable and exact,
Precise and just like Thoth.
My step is firm,
My advice excellent,
I am a thinker who has taught himself what must be
known.

Stele of Intef

If you know the wisdom of the Sage you do not attack it,
No misfortune happens around him.

Merikare

Do not make a Sage intervene in a trivial matter when a
more important one awaits. Do not let a fool intervene in
an important matter or you will then have to appeal to a
Sage.

Ankh-Sheshonk

The carrot and the stick are used equally by the wise
man.

Insinger Papyrus

When a wise man is put to the test he is hardly conscious
of his spiritual achievements.

Ankh-Sheshonk

He who has been chosen out of the crowd is not automatically a wise man because of that.

Ankh-Sheshonk

I have accomplished four perfect acts at the Gates of
Heaven.
I have created the four winds so that all men can breathe
wherever they may find themselves: this is one of my
acts.
I have created the great annual flood so the poor and rich
can benefit equally: this is one of my acts.
I have created all men equal but I have never commanded disorder. Their hearts have disobeyed my commands. This is one of my acts.
I have made mankind so that their hearts will never forget the West so that they may continue to sacrifice to the
Gods: this is one of my acts.

Texts of the Sarcophagi, VII

Act for the sake of God and He will act for you.

Merikare

Happy are they who heed the words of God, for their
plans will never go wrong.

Temple of Redeseyeh

Thoth, the God of Knowledge, rewards every act according to its own merit.

Petosiris

A just action comes around again since we have been
commanded :
Act for he who acts
So that he is committed to his action.

Stories of the Oases

The reward for those who act
Is that one will act for them.
This is the Law in the heart of God.

Inscription of Neferhotep, XII Dynasty

As you act so shall you be treated.
To speak a good word is to build a monument.

Petosiris

A man in public office must be skilled at his job, in the
same way as a well has to be rich in water for it to be
drawn upon.

Amenemope

Do not throw a spear if your aim is poor.

Ankh-Sheshonk

Do not dip your nib in ink to do harm to a man.
The finger of the scribe is like the beak of the ibis.
Take care not to misuse it.

Amenemope

Do not allow the ignorant man and the fool to do work
for which they are unsuited.

Ankh-Sheshonk

Never reply angrily to a superior. Know how to back
down and say soothing words while he rants and raves.
It is a remedy which will calm his heart.

Ani

Do not push yourself forward when your superior enters
in case you bring harm upon your name.
If you suffer a reproach, do not speak and keep quiet
until the situation improves.

Ani

What a perfect day!
Heaven works for our hearts.
That which we love is our work.

Tomb of Paheri

A lazy man never gets around to doing anything.
He who knows how to make plans is worthy of consid-
eration.

Ani

If you never do the work that needs doing, the field will
never get ploughed.

Ani

Do not say: 'I have ploughed the field but haven't been
paid in return.'
Plough it again, it's good to work.

Ankh-Sheshonk

8

Wisdom and Power

It is those who work who produce food.
If the household goes hungry, its foundations are weakened.

The Loyalist Teaching

I am truly a dignitary with a great heart,
Sweet-natured and friendly.
I am neither negligent nor lazy.
It was my heart which gained me my high office,
It was the way I acted and lived that put me in the first rank.
I am a being of worth created by God.

Stele of Rediou-Khnum

Pharaoh

The Pharaonic institution is the perfect way to govern.

Merikare

He who rules over the Two Lands is a wise man. As Master of the nobility, Pharaoh cannot be an ignorant man.
He was already wise at his mother's breast,
Since God has chosen him from millions of men.

Merikare

The companions of Pharaoh are the Gods.

Merikare

Pharaoh is unique and Pharaoh is efficient,
There is none like him.
His projects follow the steps of the ibis.
His insights are those of a master of knowledge.
He rejoices in justice,
Thanks to Ptah, the heart is gladdened.

Group Statue of Horemheb and Queen Mut-Nedjemet,
Museum of Turin

The language of Pharaoh is what directs him, steering the ship of righteousness.

Texts of the Pyramids, 1306c

Thanks to Pharaoh, who turns the ignorant toward wisdom, the common people can surpass the great, and the last become the first.

The Teaching of a Man to His Son

Pharaoh is a vital power.
His word is prosperity.
He creates that which is.
He who respects his life will not commit evil actions,
He whom Pharaoh loves will become an honoured being.

Sehetep-Ib-Re

Ra, the divine light, has placed Pharaoh on the earth for ever.
In order to judge men and satisfy the Gods,
That he might execute justice and shun evil.
Pharaoh sacrifices to the Gods and gives offerings to the immortals.

Assmann, Maat, p.117

Pharaoh is he who increases wealth and knows how to give.
Pharaoh is the lord of joy.
He who rebels against him would pull down Heaven.

Merikare

Become brothers in your heart with His Majesty.
He is the creative spark that lies in our hearts.
His eyes see everything.
He is the divine light thanks to whose rays we can see.

The Loyalist Teaching

Pharaoh is subsistence,
His mouth is food.

The Loyalist Teaching

Pharaoh is the canal which governs the flow of the river,
The cool room where man finds rest,
The rampart on the walls of heavenly metal,
The refuge whose power is constant,
A haven of peace which shelters the man menaced by his enemies,
The shelter in the time of flood,
Cool, fresh water in the blazing heat,
A dry and warm place in the winter,
The mountain that blocks the wind and storm,
The power which stops the enemy at the borders.

Hymn to Sesostris III (Kahun Papyrus)

Pharaoh has united the heavens.
Pharaoh has built the city of God as was his duty.
Pharaoh has become the Trinity.

Texts of the Pyramids, 514

Pharaoh is charitable through the works that he does for the Gods by building temples and fashioning their images.

Amada Stele

O ye who dwell on this earth,
Pay tribute to the Pharaoh,
That you may live.
Guard his work,
Protect what he commands.
This deed will be beneficial to he who does it,
He will be venerated, loved by his God.
He will thus be complete.
His bearing will be perfect throughout his life.

Relief of Metjetji

Pharaoh, your eyes are the eyes of the Gods,
It is you who gives light to the whole country,
Who disperses the darkness for the human race.

Brooklyn Papyrus II

The Art of Government

For men, God has created leaders capable of leading,
supports to strengthen the backbone of the weak.

Merikare

Powerful is he whose nobles are great.
Powerful is the Pharaoh whose servants are competent,
Venerable is he who is rich in noble beings.

Merikare

Grant your ministers the necessary importance
To carry out your commands.
Those who are at ease in their work will never be partial,
Since they have wealth and lack for nothing.
An impoverished man will never conduct himself right-
eously,
And as for those who say:
'Oh, if only I was rich!'
They will never know how to be just,
Since they will favour those who will grant them their
desire.

Merikare

If you are a guide in charge of a large number of people,
Look for any occasion to display efficiency,
So that your way of governing may be without fault.

Ptah-Hotep

Never let an ungodly or a mediocre man give orders to
people.

Ankh-Sheshonk

God leaves town when it is governed by a bad ruler.

Ankh-Sheshonk

When Ra, the divine light, is angry with a country, law,
justice and values break down and fools take the place of
wise men.

Ankh-Sheshonk

Have no confidence in your brother,
Know no friends,
Do not have intimates,
There is nothing useful in that.
Since a man has no friends on the day of misfortune.

Amenemhat I

Power is exercised thanks to intuitive knowledge.

Texts of the Pyramids, 300c

Let a leader not brag about being a powerful man,
Since there is no power without the presence of Amon,
the hidden God.
It is He who makes the weak strong.

Stele of Piankhi

Do not use the power of God for yourself,
As if neither destiny nor fate existed.

Amenemope

If you are powerful,
Act so that you may be respected,
As a function of knowledge and calm language.
Do not give orders unless circumstances demand them.

Ptah-Hotep

Do not use force.
If you do, force will be used against you.

Papyrus in the Louvre, 2414

Do not boast of your strength.
That would be to be unaware of what will happen
And what punishment God will inflict.

Kagemni

The crocodile makes no noise.
However, one fears him for a long time.

Amenemope

9

Wisdom and Human Relationships

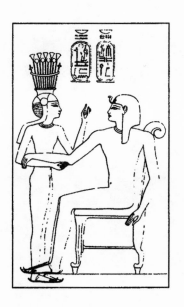

Humanity

God has created man with the tears of His eyes.

Ostracon Cairo 25207

God has provided a sanctuary for man.
When they cry He listens.

Merikare

Mankind, the flock of God, is well provided for.
He has created Heaven and Earth for their hearts,
He has driven off the dangerous creature that lives in the water,
He has created breath that their noses may breathe,
They are in His image, issuing from His body.
He rises in the heavens for them,
He has created plants, cattle, poultry and fish to feed them,
But He has exterminated His enemies and punished their children
Because they had thought of rebelling against Him.

Merikare

Do not join a crowd that you meet when it has gathered to fight.
Keep away from rebels.

Ani

May mankind perish so that silence can return to the earth and the clamour cease.

Ipu-Or

The Ancient Ones

Keep to the teaching of the Ancients, to those who came
before you.
Their words are lost in their books.
Open them,
Read and copy their knowledge,
Since only a being who knows how to learn becomes
skilful.

Merikare

Mothers

Words are spoken by the mother, mistress of Heaven,
Queen of all the Gods:
She gives life, stability and prosperity as her gifts.

Abu Simbel, Temple of Nefertari

Your mother is Heaven.
She stretches out over you.
You enter through her mouth,
You leave between her thighs like the sun, every day.

Sarcophagus of Ankh-Nefer-Ib-Re

Give back in abundance the bread that your mother gave
you.
Support her as she supported you.
She did plenty for you who were a burden to her,
Without saying:
'Don't bother me any more.'
For three years she suckled you,
And her heart did not sink at your excrement.
She sent you to school each day so that you could learn
to write,
And each day she watched over you.

Ani

Parents and Family

Pour out the water of libation for your father and mother
Who rest in the valley of death.
The Gods will bear witness to this just act.

Ani

The family of the just will be reunited in the hereafter:
Father, mother, friends, companions, children, wife and
servants
And all his wealth and goods.
This has been shown to be true millions of times.

Texts of the Sarcophagi, Ch.146

Woman

A woman with a happy heart brings equilibrium.

Ptah-Hotep

If a woman is at peace with her husband, things will never go wrong.

Ankh-Sheshonk

The woman who looks after the house well is an irreplaceable treasure.

Insinger Papyrus

Do not exercise control over your wife in her house when well you know how efficient she is.
Do not say to her:
'Where's that thing gone? Go and get it!'
When she has put whatever it is in its correct place.
Observe her with admiration and keep quiet,
So that you can make sure of her energy.
When her hand is in yours, that's happiness.

Ani

Love your wife with passion.
Feed her,
Clothe her,
Oil is good for her body.
Ease her heart throughout your long life together.
She is a fertile land, she shines for her master.

Ptah-Hotep

When a man smells pleasantly of myrrh, his wife is like a cat before him.
But when a man is hurt, his wife is there like a lionness to protect him.

Ankh-Sheshonk

If you want friendship to last in a home where you enter,
Whether as a master, as a brother or as a friend,
Or in any place that you often visit,
Guard against approaching women (in a physical way).
The result is never good.
The sight of he who enters a house is never sharp enough to do this well.
Thousands of men are thus diverted from what is good for them,
Letting themselves fall into the trap of seduction.
A brief instant of pleasure is similar to a dream,
And death awaits you if you sleep with seductresses!
As for those who end up continually lusting after women,
None of their plans will succeed.

Ptah-Hotep

Scorn the woman who has a bad reputation in your town.
Do not look at her as she passes,
Do not try to sleep with her.
A woman whose husband is far away is deep and dangerous water.
'I am gorgeous,' she tells herself daily,
When there is nobody around.
And you risk falling into her nets.

Ani

Isis, Creator of the universe,
Sovereign of the sky and the stars,
Mistress of life,
Regent of the Gods,
Magician with divine wisdom,
Female sun,
Who stamps everything with her royal seal!
Man lives on your order,
Nothing happens without your agreement.

Temple of Philae

Great of love,
With a beautiful face,
Ravishing,
Queen of charm,
Who has satisfied the divinity because of her beauty,
She has the voice of the enchantress when she sings,
She fills the palace with the scent of her perfume,
The Queen of all women,
The Mistress of the Two Lands and of all the earth.

Titles of the Queens of Egypt

I have created this work with a heart full of love for Amon.
Initiated into his secrets of origin,
Instructed through his beneficial power,
I have not forgotten what he has ordained.
My Majesty recognises his divinity.
I have acted on his orders,
It is he who has guided me,
I have never planned anything contrary to his actions,
It is he who has guided me.
I have never slept,
Because I was preoccupied with his temple.
I have never turned away from what he has commanded.
My heart was intuitively before his father,
I have entered intimately into the plans of his heart.
I have never turned my back on the city of the Master of Totality,
But rather I have turned my face toward Him.

Obelisk of Queen Hatshepsut at Karnak

All that Queen Nefertari asked for has been done.
All reality exists as a function of her desire for knowledge.
All her words brought joy to people's faces,
To hear her voice is to live.

Temple of Luxor

You are unique,
The beloved,
The incomparable,
The most beautiful woman in the world,
Like a star shining at New Year,
At the threshold of a beautiful year,
Whose grace shines out,
Whose skin glows,
With a clear look,
With sweet lips,
With a long neck,
With hair like lapis lazuli,
With fingers like the petals of the lotus,
With slim hips,
And noble carriage.

A Song of Love

His wife, his lover, is the Queen of grace, sweet in love with a helpful word, agreeable in conversation, a useful adviser in her writings: all that passes her lips is worthy of Maat; a perfect woman with a high reputation in the city, giving a helping hand to all, speaking of what is good, repeating what is loved, giving pleasure to all: listening to her one never learns evil, she who is beloved by all, she whose name is Renpet-Neferet,
'the Perfect Year'.

Text on the tomb of Petosiris describing the wife of the Sage

Children

Marry a woman when you are young,
And let her have children while you are young.

Ani

How wonderful is a son who obeys his father!
How happy he is of whom it is said:
'A son is kind-natured when he knows how to listen.'

Ptah-Hotep

Can you create a spiritual son with the grace of God.
If he is righteous,
If he conforms to your values,
And if he takes care of your goods as well,
Shower him with gifts.
He is indeed your true son.
He carries the seed of your kin, of your soul.
Do not let your hearts be sundered.
But the seed of a man can engender conflict.
If your son goes wrong,
If he ignores your advice,
If he is disobedient and insolent to all that you say,
If he is rude and contemptuous,
Drive him away.
He is not your son.

Ptah-Hotep

All will go well for the man whose household is numer-
ous.

Ani

Do not blame those who are childless,
Do not criticise them for not having any,
And do not boast about having them yourself.
There are plenty of fathers in trouble,
And similarly lots of mothers in trouble,
So a childless woman can be more content than they.

Ptah-Hotep

Friendship

Distance yourself from the rebel,
Do not make a friend of him.
Make friends with the just and righteous man whose
actions you have observed.

Ani

You do not know the heart of your brother so well as
when you do not ask him for help in a moment of difficulty.

Insinger Papyrus

The House

Build your own home for yourself and do not assume
that your parents' house will come to you by right.

Ani

Do not dwell in a house that has been cursed by God. Its capacity for destruction will turn on you.

Ankh-Sheshonk

10

The Qualities of the Sage

Love

When Pharaoh loves, he creates.
When Pharaoh hates, he does not create.

Texts of the Pyramids, 412b

It's thanks to the love that supports you that your work
will last.

Merikare

Give your love to the whole world,
Since a happy personality is remembered
When the years have long rolled by.

Merikare

Good Character

A good character is a sheltering sky for a human being.

Merikare

Honesty

Till your own field and you will find what you need.
A single bushel of what God has given you is better than
five thousand bushels that have been dishonestly
obtained.

Amenemope

Do not falsify the scales,
Do not alter the weights,
Do not lessen the fractions that are used for measuring.

Amenemope

What is the point of being expensively dressed if you
behave like a fraud before God?
Crockery disguised as gold is revealed as lead in the light
of day.

Amenemope

Impartiality

Bias is an abomination in the sight of God.
Act towards a stranger as you would to he who is close
to you.

Tomb of Rekhmire

Humility

May your heart never be vain because of what you know.
Take counsel from the ignorant as well as the wise,
Since one never reaches the limits of art,
And there has never been an artisan who has attained
perfection.

Ptah-Hotep

Do not scorn a little thing,
For fear of suffering from it.

Ankh-Sheshonk

A little worry can break your back,
A little good news can make your heart leap,
A little dew can make the grass live,
A little bee can make honey.

Ankh-Sheshonk

Self-Criticism

Know how to be critical of yourself to avoid the criticism of others.

Hor-Djedef

Discretion

Do not enter someone else's house before they permit it and welcome you in.
Do not let your eye be too curious.
Know how to look silently,
And do not gossip about someone who isn't there.
It would be a serious fault if your stories were listened to.

Ani

Do not pour your heart out to people,
Do not associate with those who bare their souls.

Amenemope

Obedience

Your back is not going to break just because it is bending.

Amenemope

Respect

Know how to inspire fear and make yourself respected.
He who is held in awe is a good judge.
But the true function of the judge is to practise justice.
If you fear him too much then there must be something wrong with you.

Tomb of Rekhmire

Show respect for the lives of those who are frank.

Merikare

Do not hurt those older than you,
Since they have seen the divine light before you.

Amenemope

Do not laugh at the blind,
Do not torment a dwarf,
Do not make the situation of a cripple even more painful,
Do not torment a man who is in the hands of God,
Do not get annoyed with his mistakes.

Amenemope

Generosity

The riches of the generous man are greater than those of the miser.

Ankh-Sheshonk

Be a father to your subordinates,
Instruct the young,
Help the unfortunate,
Provide for those in need,
Protect the orphan and the widow,
Open your ears to those who tell the truth,
Keep away from evil people.

Baken-Khonsu

I have built my house perfectly,
So that its doors were wide and welcoming.
To those who wanted them,
I have offered presents,
I have shown myself generous to those both near and far,
Since I wanted my name respected in the mouths of those
who live on this earth.

Stele in Cairo 20543

Those who like to give food to others will find a welcome at table in every house.

Ankh-Sheshonk

Do not eat bread without giving some to those near you
who do not have anything to eat.
Since the bread is eternal while man does not last.

Ani

If you find a poor man crushed by a heavy debt, break it
down into three parts. Cancel two parts but maintain the
third. You will thus be on the right path of life.

Amenemope

Conviviality

A man loses nothing by speaking pleasantly,
His discourse gains nothing if it is disagreeable.

Amenemope

Do not neglect to help those who help you.

Ankh-Sheshonk

Politeness

Do not sit down when there is a person standing who is
older than you or whose rank is higher than yours.

Ani

Happiness and Joy

Happiness is to be found in observing righteousness (Maat).

Petosiris

You will know happiness if your life is lived within the limits set by the will of God.

Ani

Understand, Pharaoh is the master of the greatness of the heart.

Merikare

There is no evil in me.
That is why I have taken possession of heaven and earth.
Joy has been given to me.
I have known abundance.

Texts of the Sarcophagi, Ch.468

I have risen up to heaven,
I have realised my desire,
I have attained mastery,
Joy has been given me.

Texts of the Sarcophagi, Ch.468

How wonderful it is to see,
How happy are they who understand!

Texts of the Pyramids, 1980a, 1943b

How marvellous it is when the boats descend the river and there are no thieves!
How marvellous it is when the tombs are maintained,
When the mummies are in good condition,
When the paths are safe for walking.
How wonderful when the hands of men built the Pyramids,
When reservoirs are dug,
When plantations of sycamores are planted for the Gods.
When men drink to fullness,
And their hearts are content.
When all mouths express joy,
When a simple meal in the shade satisfies the needs of all.

Ipu-Or

Every new dawn brings me more joy, from my young childhood up to the great age that I have reached, in the interior of the temple of the Hidden God. I have seen Him everywhere where my eyes have the ability to still see His sacred face.

Bakhen-Khonsu

Make today a happy day,
Wear garlands of flowers and of lotus,
While your wife, the lover of your heart, is sitting next to you.
Forget your troubles, dream of happiness.
Until that day comes when you embark on the ship that will carry you to the country of silence.

Song of the Harpist

Misfortune

Misfortune is a son as an enemy, a brother as an adversary, a man who murders his father, each mouth full of 'Love me'.

Hermitage Papyrus 1116

Wealth

God gives riches, the sage looks after them and he knows how to get them without being greedy.

Insinger Papyrus

Do not place any confidence in your heart in the accumulation of riches,
Since everything that you have is a gift from God.

Ptah-Hotep

Do not exhaust yourself looking for wealth.
Be satisfied with what you have.

Amenemope

Look at what is in the bowl in front of you and let that
satisfy your needs.

Amenemope

Think of living in peace with what you possess,
And whatever the Gods choose to give will come of its
own accord.

Ptah-Hotep

The wealth of a city is a righteous governor.
The wealth of a temple is a good priest.
The wealth of a field is the time when the land is worked.
The wealth of a store is when goods are stocked.
The wealth of a household is a wise woman.
The wealth of a sage is his words.
The wealth of a workman is his tools.

Ankh-Sheshonk

Poverty from the hand of God is better than riches in a
warehouse,
Eating a simple cake with a peaceful heart is better than
riches accumulated with worry.

Amenemope

Do not make a difference between rich and poor but
value people acccording to how they act.

Merikare

He who was rich last year could well be poor this year.

Ani

God prefers those who honour the poor to those who venerate the rich.

Amenemope

If you make money, give some to God. It is reserved for the poor.

Ankh-Sheshonk

Do not build yourself a ferry with the sole idea of making a profit. Charge the full price of passage from the rich and let the poor travel free.

Amenemope

The rewards of the unjust do not last long and their children will inherit nothing,

The Loyalist Teaching

Foresight

It is the pilot who looks ahead who will not capsize his boat.

Amenemope

11

Faults to Avoid

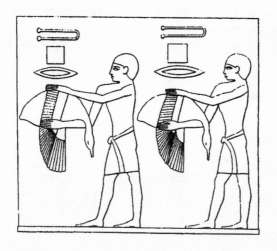

Greed

If you want your conduct to be good,
Deliver yourself from all evil.
Fight greed in your heart on all occasions.
Greed is the serious illness of the incurable.
Curing it is impossible.
Greed spreads unhappiness among mothers and fathers,
And among the brothers of the mother.
It divides husband and wife.
Greed is a reunion for all sorts of evil,
It is like a sack that contains everything that is hateful.

Ptah-Hotep

The greedy man fails.
What he meets is checkmate.
There is no yesterday for the lazy,
No friends for those deaf to righteousness,
No feast days for the rapacious.

Stories of the Oases

Acquiring things with greed is an evil that has no end.

Ankh-Sheshonk

Desiring the goods of another is a form of madness.

Merikare

Do not fill your heart with desire for the goods of others but rather concern yourself with what you have built up yourself.

Ani

It is greed that leads to quarrels and fighting in a household and brings unhappiness to families.

Ankh-Sheshonk

Do not be rapacious even when you have to act against someone who is himself rapacious.

Stories of the Oases

The rewards of greed are as ash blown on the wind.

Ankh-Sheshonk

Do not hold back a part of what should go to the temple,
Do not be greedy,
Do not turn a servant away from God.

Kha-Keper-Re-Seneb

Vanity

The vain man is lost by his own heart,
Like a tree that grows too tall is pruned.

Insinger Papyrus

He who spits at Heaven,
His spit will fall back down on him.

Ankh-Sheshonk

Pettiness

The mean-spirited person will never get anywhere.
The Loyalist Teaching

Malice

The goods of a wise man are lost if he gives way to spite.
Insinger Papyrus

Keep your distance from those with hate in their hearts.
Ankh-Sheshonk

Do not associate with wicked people because of their reputation.

Insinger Papyrus

The death of an evil man is a cause for celebration for those he leaves behind.

Ankh-Sheshonk

Violence and Excess

The man of excess does not practise righteousness.
The man whose heart gets carried away is not the man
who is looked for when action is needed.

Stories of the Oases

A storm that rages like a fire in straw:
That is what the angry man is like.
Keep away from him, leave him alone.
God knows how to deal with him.

Amenemope

Do not protest to those who provoke you,
Do not reply to them.
He who does evil,
The land will reject him,
And the flood will carry him away.

Amenemope

Physical violence calls for retaliation,
Everything it accomplishes will be caught up in this.

Merikare

Do not steal from the unfortunate,
Do not be violent towards the weak.
Do not stretch out your hand to threaten the old,
And do not speak impolitely to them.

Amenemope

The hard man causes his own destruction,
No descendant will honour him.

The Loyalist Teaching

Let the quiet man become violent
Only if the altars of the Gods are desecrated,
Then God will act against those who rebel against the
temple.

Merikare

Theft

Do not steal, you will profit from this.

Amenemope

Do not move the boundary markers at the edge of a field,
Do not change the position of the measuring line.
Identify he who acts like this on the earth,
Since he is an oppressor of the weak
And an enemy dedicated to your destruction.

Amenemope

Ignorance

As for the ignorant man who does not listen,
He will accomplish nothing. . .
He is like a dead man walking through daily life.

Ptah-Hotep

Everyone can find the path to God,
But the ignorant cannot.

Ankh-Sheshonk

For the ignorant, the work of God is nothing but a joke.

Ankh-Sheshonk

Stupidity

Advice given to the stupid weighs as little as the wind.

Ankh-Sheshonk

The fool who lights a fire gets too close and burns himself.

Ankh-Sheshonk

Keeping company with the stupid brings misfortune.

Insinger Papyrus

It is better to have a serpent hanging around the house than a fool.

Ankh-Sheshonk

The wicked acts of an imbecile harm those closest to him.

Ankh-Sheshonk

You exhaust a donkey by loading it with bricks.

Ankh-Sheshonk

Credulity

Credulity leads to unhappiness.

Merikare

Negligence

If you neglect a problem it will bring a double load of difficulties.

Stories of the Oases

Lies

When a lie emerges,
It wanders and cannot cross in the ferry,
It does not travel well.
Those who become rich thanks to lies
Will leave no descendants or heirs on this earth.
Those who sail with a lie will find no berth,
And their boat will not tie up in port.

Stories of the Oases

Ingratitude

I have been generous to the poor,
I have looked after the orphan,
I have acted in a way which has brought riches to those
who possessed nothing as well as to those who were
already rich,
And it is he who has shared my food who has raised an
army against me,
And it is those to whom I have offered my hand who
have brought terror.

Amenemhat I

Chatter

Do not pour out your feelings to just anyone:
You will lose all respect this way.

Amenemope

A gossip is a disturbance in the community.

Merikare

The man who knows how to respect will prosper,
The humble man is worthy of praise.
The tent is open to the silent.
The seat of the calm man is spacious.
Do not chatter, the knives are being sharpened for the
unrighteous.

Kagemni

Slander

Do not speak against anyone, great or small: it's an insult
to the soul (Ka).

Ptah-Hotep

Do not repeat a slanderous rumour,
Do not listen to it.
It is a way of expressing oneself used by the intemperate.
Let a slanderous rumour be thrown on the dust-heap.
Do not speak about it.

Ptah-Hotep

Materialism

The heart of he who listens to his stomach is weakened.
He will provoke disdain rather than love.
He who has a great heart has a gift from God,
He who obeys his stomach obeys the enemy.

Ptah-Hotep

Pampering Oneself

Do not pamper yourself when you are young.
Otherwise when you are old you will be weak.

Ankh-Sheshonk

Gluttony

Gluttony is contemptible, you should show it the door.
A glass of water is enough to quench your thirst,
A mouthful of vegetables will strengthen your heart.
Unfortunate is he who still wants more when the meal is
over.

Kagemni

If your friends drink too much, tell them:
No alcohol for me!
If not, you will be found sprawled out on the ground as
if you were a helpless child.

Ani

12

The Destiny and Journeys of the Sage

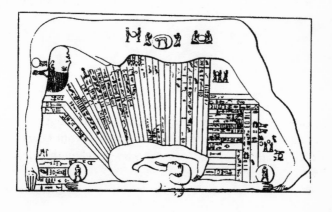

Those who the Gods guide cannot get lost.
Those they forbid passage will not be able to cross the river of life.

Ptah-Hotep

An evil fate awaits those who walk upon the waters of the Gods.
Whereas those who walk on the earth are reduced to fighting to gain a favourable destiny.

Temple of Esna

For the shining soul who advances,
The path is already there.

Ptah-Hotep

The faculty of transcendence, the *ba*, makes its way to the place that it knows.
It will not wander from its habitual path.
Thus, no magician can obstruct it.

Merikare

You will take the form of a phoenix, a swallow,
Of a heron, whichever you want.
You will cross without being fettered,
You will float upon the wave,
You will be born a second time.
Your eyes will be opened,
Your ears will be made to hear what is ordained,
Your mouth will speak,
Your feet will walk,
Your hands and your arms will move.

Tomb of Paheri

Can you leave the light of day,
Upright on two feet,
Can you exercise mastery on the Way of Light,
Since you know the secret routes.

Texts of the Sarcophagi, IV 49

I travel the Milky Way,
In the company of the Divine Light.
I have regulated my step correctly,
I rule Heaven.

Texts of the Sarcophagi II, 376 and 164

Raise Heaven to the height of your arms,
Widen the earth to the length of your stride.

The Book of Leaving the Day, Ch.48

I am a jackal with swift feet who can travel around the
world in an instant.

The 'Red Chapel' of Hatshepsut

Amon-Ra (The secret of the revelation through the light) is the
Double mast that catches the wind,
He does not waver in the north wind,
He does not flinch from the south wind.
He supports the sail,
Even if the weather is bad,
And He allows passage.

Ostracon British Museum 5656a

Venerate Amon Ra, the king of the Gods, the primordial,
He who was the first to come into existence,
The unique God, He who is loved, He who has raised the sky,
He who created the sky, the land and the waters!
Come to me, Amon,
Help me to reach the limit of the desert.
You who saves the castaway,
Help me to reach firm ground.

Theban Relief, Cairo Museum

The tempest moves aside for the sailor who remembers the name of Amon.
The storm becomes a sweet breeze for he who invokes His name.
Thus the shipwrecked mariner is saved.
Amon is more effective than millions for he who places Him in his heart.
Thanks to Him the single man becomes stronger than a crowd.

Hymn to Amon at Leyde

I am the heart of the Lord,
The eyes and ears of the King.
See, I am a captain of his ship.
I know not sleep by night and by day.
I stand up and I sit down,
My heart lies under the bonds of time before and time after.

Tomb of Rekhmire

If you work the rudder correctly,
You will be in the flow of the current which leads to the accomplishment of justice.
Keep watch so as not to undertake a voyage which would endanger the ropes of the rudder.

Stories of the Oases

I am the steering oar of the Divine Light with which Perfection, that oar which fire cannot burn and water cannot make wet, is satisfied.

Texts of the Sarcophagi V, 15b-16a

I am she who has the oar of the ship of command.
The sovereign of life,
Guide of the light on the beautiful roads,
I am she who fixes the cables on the rudders on the routes
of the West,
I am the Third,
The Queen of brightness,
The one who guides the great ones who are lost and
exhausted on the roads of the reborn.
I am she who has the splendour on the roads of the
cloudy sky.
I am the Queen of the winds on the isle of joy,
I am she who has the oars,
Who guides those who are lost in the underworld,
I am Hathor,
Queen of the northern sky,
Who watches over the reborn,
I am a haven of tranquillity for the just,
A ferry for the chosen,
I am she who has created the ship for the passage of the
just.

Texts of the Sarcophagi IV, 177

The crooked man does not enter the place of righteous-
ness,
The country of silence.
Only the man with a good heart is permitted entrance to
the ferry,
Since the ferryman does not allow the wicked to cross.
How happy they are, those who cross to the other side.

Hymn to Amon at Leyde

13

Life, Death and the After-Life

Length of Life

Amon may be so far away on His many roads,
But His eyes and His ears stay open.
He hears the cries of those who call to Him,
And in an instant He comes from afar to those who
invoke Him.
It is He who prolongs or shortens life.
He changes the destiny of those whom He loves.

Hymn to Amon at Leyde

Every man who is enlightened will reach the age of one
hundred and ten.
Ten years of his life will be without disorder, without
impurity, without faults or lies, conforming to that which
the neophyte has accomplished on the way to becoming
a sage.
That is why he will eat bread every day next to the
powerful God.

Texts of the Sarcophagi, Ch.228

Death

To hide death in the background is bad for man.

Texts of the Pyramids, 1439

When death comes, it embraces the old like a child in the arms of its mother.

Ani

The West is the dwelling place for he who has not transgressed the Rule.
Happy is he who reaches there!
Nobody can reach there unless
Their hearts have conformed exactly to the Rule.
Down there there is no distinction between rich and poor,
Unless it is in the favour of he who is found to be righteous
When weighed in the scales of justice before the master of Eternity.

Petosiris

Happy is he who reaches the West,
Then he is safe in the hands of God.

Amenemope

Death comes before me today like a cure after an illness,
Like liberty after imprisonment.
Death has come before me today like the perfume of myrrh.
Like sitting under a sail on a windy day.
Death has come before me today like the scent of the lotus,
Like being seated by the banks of rivers of ecstasy.
Death has come before me today like the moment when clamour ceases, like the moment when you finally reach home after a long expedition.
Death has come before me today like the lightening of a darkened sky, like the discovery of something unknown.
Death has come before me today like when a man longs to see his home again after years of captivity.

Dialogue of a man with his Ba spirit

The Tomb

Do not lose yourself in the exterior world to the extent that you neglect the place of your eternal rest.

Ani

Embellish your tomb in the Necropolis,
Enrich your resting place in the West.
Welcome this thought,
Since death is a narrow gate for us,
And life triumphant.
The dwelling place of death is destined for life.

Hor-Djedef

As for my tomb, this kingdom, I built it in the shade. I was respected both by men and by God. Not once did the builders use a single brick of anyone else's tomb to build mine. One remembers the judgement after death.

Inscription of Remen-Oui-Kai

The Court of the Underworld

The assembly of judges metes out justice to the condemned and you know that they will not be indulgent on the day when they do justice to he who submits to it.
And it is even more serious when the accuser is a sage!
Do not fool yourself with the length of years: to them the length of existence seems but an hour.
A man lives after his death,
And his actions are judged as a whole next to him.
It is eternity that laughs,
And you would be foolish to ignore it.
Those who reach there without committing evil,
Will be there like Gods,
They will move freely there like the Masters of Eternity.

Merikare

Life After Death

All who are knowledgeable will not die a second time.
His enemies will not be able to harm him.
No magic will keep him tied to this earth.

Texts of the Sarcophagi, Ch.83

Live life, then truly you will not die a death.

Texts of the Pyramids, 810

O Osiris the king,
You left but you returned.
You slept but you awoke.
You have landed on the banks of the underworld but yet
you live.

Texts of the Pyramids, 1975

Every fortunate person who knows the secret of Osiris
hidden in the shadows will live as a living man amongst
the living.

Texts of the Sarcophagi VII, 364

Goddess of Heaven,
Hearken to me,
Allow me to enter into the life that is yours.
Do not close the doors before me.
Allow me to cross the firmament,
Unite me with the doors of the dawn.

Texts of the Sarcophagi, Ch.644

155

My protection comes from all the Gods, eternally.
I am someone whose name is secret.
I am he who was never counted.
I am completely unharmed.

The Book of Leaving the Day, Ch.7

Place your bones in order,
Reassemble your limbs,
Turn your face towards the beautiful West:
You will return, eternally youthful, each and every day.

Texts of the Sarcophagi VII, 255

Rebirth is that which moves amongst its brothers the Gods in the country of light.

Texts of the Sarcophagi VI, 296

Give me your hands, I was born from you!
You are the Word and the intuitive knowledge,
Which are near to the creator every day.

Texts of the Sarcophagi, Ch.335

I was born from the creative power, born of herself.
She conceived me in her heart,
She created me with her magical power.
I was not born of a human childbirth.

Texts of the Sarcophagi, Ch.75

You live this wonderful life which is that of the Master of the Country of Light, of the great wave that lies in the heavens.

Texts of the Pyramids, 1772

May my name last like the stars in the skies,
Let them buttress my statue like one of their followers,
Let my creative power be remembered in his temple night and day,
May my youth be renewed like the moon,
Let my name not be obliterated by eternity.

Statue in Cairo, 42237

Paradise and the After-Life

I have not neglected the day of crossing to the other world,
I am remembered by those who rest in their eternal dwelling places.
I have acted in a way that will leave them to feast in joy.
Thus have I arrived in the realm of the hereafter with the favour of the Gods.

Statue in Cairo, 42231

Fear does not exist in the afterlife.
There are no arguments.
There, people do not doubt one another,
In this country that knows no discord.

Theban tomb of Neferhotep

Plan to find yourself in the land of plenty amongst the followers of Osiris and among the servants of Thoth. Each day they eat bread with the living, they do not die, they breathe the breath of immortality.

Texts of the Sarcophagi, Ch.1162

Think about the countryside, the towns, the land, the tilling and the harvesting, seeing the Divine Light, Ra, and Osiris, the reborn, and Thoth, knowledge, every day. You will have the mastery of water and air, doing everything that you love like he who finds himself on the isle of fire, then life will be such that death is impossible, dwelling in the land of plenty where there are fields and pastures for always and forever.

Texts of the Sarcophagi, Ch.467

The south wind changes to the north for you.
Your mouth is guided to the teat of the celestial cow.
You become pure enough to look at the sun.
You cleanse yourself in the divine basin.
You are strong beside Osiris, the rebirth.
Come in total silence to the vital power.

The Song of the Harpist

You are the mistress of your conscience,
Of your heart,
Of your arms and legs.
You consume your funerary offerings.
You are the mistress of the water, of the air, of the fecund flood, of the twin banks,
Of those who would act against you in the Kingdom of the Underworld.
You are not nourished by earthly food.

Texts of the Sarcophagi, Ch.225

The Being of Light

The being of light is destined for heaven.

Texts of the Pyramids, 474

Give a lot to the spirit of light,
Do what it loves.

Ani

I have explored heaven,
I have gone deeply into the country of light,
I have crossed the light,
I have walked its length,
I have become master of the spiritual power of my predecessor,
I am truly a being of light.

Texts of the Sarcophagi, Ch.574

The Ba, the Spirit-Bird

A man must accomplish what is useful and sacred to his
Ba.

Merikare

I have come to you, master of the sacred land.
I have practised the Law on earth, without deviation;
Allow me to be glorified in Heaven and powerful on the
earth.
Made just like the masters of the starry constellations.
Let the ability to move myself (*ba*) allow me to travel to
anywhere I wish.

Stele of Rome at Abydos

Your faculty of movement or *ba* will live forever,
Like Orion set in the navel of the Goddess of Heaven.
You will become as gold,
You will shine brilliantly.
In the constellations of the stars you will fulfil a royal
function.
Your name will be great in the West.

Ritual of Embalming

14

The Temple and its Rites

Building

God was created before Heaven and earth existed.
So the world still finds itself in an ocean of primordial
energy.
He has raised the heavenly vault and rolled out the earth.

Arena at Toura

God has made me to do for Him what has to be done and
what He has commanded me to accomplish.

Sesostris I

Build monuments to God:
These will make the names of the builders live on.

Merikare

The Temple

Turn your gaze to this temple where His Majesty has put you.
He sails Heaven while overseeing it.
He is content when His Rule is respected.

A Rule of Edfu

The sky will be so established on its four supports,
That the earth will be stable on its foundations,
Ra will shine by day and the moon will shine by night,
Orion will be the manifestation of Osiris
And Sirius the Queen of the stars,
The flood will come at its appointed time
And the earth will bring forth plants,
The north wind will blow favourably,
And the priests will do their duty
And the stars will rest in their proper places,
The temple will be stable like Heaven.

Temple of Kom Ombo

The master buider constructs a temple whose peak is as high as heaven.
The sun rises through the love of it.

Abu Simbel

In its village, the temple is like Heaven.

Temple of Sahoure

The doors to Heaven are open,
The doors of the temple are unbolted.
The house is ready for its master:
Let them leave when they want to leave,
Let them enter when they want to enter.

Ritual of the Opening of the Mouth

Celebrate the service of the pure priest each month,
Wear white sandals,
Join with the temple,
Penetrate the mysteries,
Enter into the secret sanctuary,
Eat bread within the temple.

Merikare

Rites, Festivals and Offerings

To be the master of the life which is renewed eternally,
your name must be:
He who lives the rites.

Second Book of Breaths

Celebrate the festival of your God and repeat the ceremony at the right time.

Ani

Since the festival of the months,
Of the festival of the sixth day,
Of the festival of the half-month,
Of the grand procession,
Of the rising of Sothis,
Of the feast of the dead,
Of the feast of Thoth,
Of the feast of the first birth,
Of the birth of Isis,
Of the procession of Min, God of fertility,
Of the procession of the funeral priests,
Of the evening rest,
Of the rising of the river,
Since the festivals of Heaven have their appointed day,
In accordance with tradition,
You will dress in a robe of fine linen and clothes worn by
the body of God,
You will be anointed with oil,
You shall drink water from the cup of the altar.

Tomb of Paheri

According to the offerings of Pharaoh and Anubis, he
who finds himself on the mountain which dominates the
divine chapel and the place of resurrection, the master of
the sacred earth.
He can be permitted to reach a great age and wealth,
To be buried in the West,
To become honoured alongside the Great God,
To walk peacefully along the perfect roads of the West,
And to be raised to God, Master of Heaven.
Let Pharaoh make known to you the transfiguration
through the rites, from each sacred festival.

Tomb of Hirkhouf

Act in a way that the offering may be abundant and the
bread uncountable.
Increase the daily offerings.
This is a worthy act and beneficial to he who does it.

Merikare

Make your offerings with what you find in your hands.
If you have nothing,
Make your offering with words.

Stele in Cairo 20003

I shall define it for you,
I shall make you know it:
Pronounce the ritual of offering. Do not make the offer-
ing small and also make no difficulties.
The rite allows no differences with others,
It does not constrain those in need.
It is an agreeable and elevating discourse,
It will be good for you to say it.

Tomb of Paheri

When the divine offerings descend,
The face of man lights up,
The hearts of the Gods are full of joy.

Texts of the Pyramids, 1554

IN THE TIME OF THE SAGES

Remember the rites held in the chapel, the incense, the offerings of water in a chalice for the ritual of the morning;
Remember the contributions of fatted geese and hens and the presentation of the divine offerings to the Gods;
Remember the sacred food prepared by the priest and the specially baked white loaves;
Remember the raising of masts and the tables of sculptured offerings.
Remember the purified priests cleansing the temples, making them white as milk,
Remember the sweetness of perfume in the country of the light and the purification of the offerings;
Above all remember to observe the Rule, and observe correctly the ritual moments.

Ipu-Or

Bibliography

H. Brunner, *Die Weisheitsbücher der Ägypter*, Munich 1991, provides a translation of many of the texts relating to wisdom and a detailed bibliography. See also M. Lichtheim, *Ancient Egyptian Literature*, 3 volumes, Berkeley-Los Angeles-London 1975–1980; A. Barucq and F. Daumas, *Hymnes et prières de L'Égypte ancienne*, Paris 1980.

On the theme of wisdom see *Les Sagesses du Proche-Orient ancien*, Paris 1963; R.J. Williams, The Sages of Ancient Egypt in the Light of Recent Scholarship. *Journal of Ancient Oriental Studies* 101, 1981, 1–19; N. Shupak, *Where can Wisdom be found? The Sage's Language in the Bible and Ancient Egyptian Literature* (*A.E.L*), Fribourg-Göttingen 1993.

The bibliography for the main texts quoted is as follows:

Amenemhat (The teaching of Amenemhat to his son Sesostris I)

— Helck W., *Der Text der 'Lehre Amenemhets I fur seinen Sohn'*, Wiesbaden 1969

— Lichtheim M., *AEL* I 135–139.
— Goedicke H., *Studies in 'The Instructions of King Amenemhat I for his son'*, 2 vol, San Antonio 1988.
— Brunner H., *Die Weisheitsbücher*, 169–177.

Amenemope
— Lange H.O., *Das Weisheitsbuch des Amenemope, aus dem papyrus 10.474 des British Museum*, 1925.
— Griffith F., The teaching of Amenophis the son of Kanakht, *Journal of Egyptian Archaeology* 12, 1926.
— Grumach I., *Untersuchungen zur Lebenslehrer des Amenemope*, Munich 1972.
— Lichtheim M., *AEL* II, 146–163.
— Brunner H., *Die Weisheitsbücher*, 231–233.

Ani
— Suys E., *La sagesse d'Ani*, Rome 1935.
— Lichtheim M., *AEL* II, 135–146.
— Brunner H., *Die Weisheitsbücher*, 196–214.
— Quack J., *Die Lehren des Ani*, Fribourg-Göttingen 1994.

Ankh-Sheshonk
— Lichtheim M., *AEL* III, 159–184.
— Brunner H., *Die Weisheitsbücher*, 257–291.

Stories of the Oases
— Vogelsang F., *Kommentar zu den Klagen des Bauern*, Hildesheim 1964.
— Lefebvre G., *Romans et contes égyptiens de l'époque pharaonique*, Paris 1976.
— Parkinson R.B., *The Tale of the Eloquent Peasant*, Oxford 1991.

Loyalist Teaching
— Posener G., *L'enseignement loyaliste. Sagesse égyptienne du Moyen Empire*, Paris 1976.
— Brunner H., *Die Weisheitsbücher*, 178–184.

Hor-Jedef
— Helck W., *Die Lehre des Djedefhour und die Lehre eines Vaters an Seinem Sohn*, Wiesbaden 1984.
— Brunner H., *Die Weisheitsbücher*, 101–103.

Ipu-Or
— Gardiner A.H., *The Admonitions of an Egyptian Sage*, Hildesheim 1969.
— Faulkner R.O., The Admonitions of an Egyptian Sage, *Journal of Egyptian Archaeology* 51, 1965.
— Lichtheim M., *AEL* I, 149–163.
— Helck W., Die 'Admonitions' Pap. Leiden, Wiesbaden 1995.

Kagemni
— Lichtheim M., *AEL* I, 59–61.
— Brunner H., *Die Weisheitsbücher*, 133–136.

Kha-Kheper-Re-Seneb
— Kadish G.E., British Museum Writing Board 5645: The Complaints of Kha-Keper-Re-Senebu, *Journal of Egyptian Archaeology* 59, 1973, 77–90.
— Lichtheim M., *AEL* I, 145–149.
— Chappaz J.L., Un manifeste littéraire du Moyen Empire. Les Lamentations de Kha-Khéper-rê-séneb, *Bulletin de la société égyptologique de Geneve* No 2, 1979, 3–12.

Book of Leaving the Day
— Barguet P., *Le Livre des Morts des anciens Égyptiens*, Paris 1967.

171

Merikare
— Lichtheim M., *AEL* I, 97–109.
— Helck W., *Die Lehre für König Merikare*, Wiesbaden 1977.
— Brunner H., *Die Weisheitsbücher*, 137–154.
— Quack J.F., *Studien zur Lehre für Merikare*, Wiesbaden 1992.

Papyrus Brooklyn
— Jasnow R., *A Late Period Hieratic Wisdom Text*, Chicago 1992.

Papyrus Insinger
— Lexa F., *Les enseignements moraux d'un scribe égyptien*, Paris 1926.
— Lichtheim M., *AEL* III, 184–217.
— Brunner H., *Die Weisheitsbücher*, 295–349.

Petosiris
— Lefebvre G., *Annales du Service des antiquités de l'Égypte*, XX, 1920, 41–121 and 207–236; XXI, 1921, 40–60, 145–162 and 222–246; XXII, 1922, 33–48 and 139–156.

Ptah-Hotep
— Žaba Z., *Les Maximes de Ptahhotep*, Prague 1956.
— Brunner H., *Die Weisheitsbücher*, 104–132.
— Lichtheim M., *AEL* I, 61–60.
— Jacq C., *L'enseignement du sage égyptien Ptah-Hotep. Le plus ancien livre du monde*, 1993.

Texts of the Pyramids
— Faulkner R.O., *The Ancient Egyptian Pyramid Texts*. Oxford 1969.

Texts of the Sarcophagi
— Faulkner R.O., *The Ancient Egyptian Coffin Texts*. Warminster 1973–78.
— Barguet P., *Textes des Sarcophages égyptiens du Moyen Empire*, Paris 1986.

Glossary

Amenemhat:
Pharaoh, father of Sesostris I.

Amon:
The King of the Gods and the father of the Pharaohs. His centre of worship was Thebes, Luxor and Karnak.

Ani:
A middle-ranking civil servant of the New Kingdom, c.1558–1085 BC.

Ankh-Sheshonk:
Sage, later jailed for political reasons.

Atum:
A God of the setting sun and the sun before dawn. He fathered the first of the Gods. His centre of worship was Heliopolis.

Ba:
Part of the soul in the shape of a bird that is set free on death.

Ennead:
A union of nine Gods. The Great Ennead of Heliopolis

consisted of Ra, Shu, Tenefet, Geb, Nut, Osiris, Isis, Seth and Nephthys.

Hathor:
The Goddess of happiness and love. She also looks after the souls of the dead. She was the wife of Horus and her sacred animal was the cow.

Hor-Jedef:
Son of the Pharaoh Cheops, who ruled in the time of the Old Kingdom, c. 2613–2494 BC.

Horus:
God of the sun, represented with the head of a falcon. Horus was also one of the titles of the Pharaohs.

Ka:
The soul or life-force that was created with a person and lives on after death.

Kagemni:
A vizier of Snefru, founder of the 4th Dynasty, c. 2613–2494 BC.

Karnak:
Large concentration of temples in upper Egypt in Luxor.

Maat:
The Goddess of truth and justice. Her symbol was a feather and after death a person's actions on earth were weighed against this feather.

Mastaba:
The inner part of an ancient Egyptian tomb.

Merikare:
A Pharaoh.

Nefertari:
Wife of Ramses II, 1290–1224 BC.

Osiris:
God of the reborn.

Ptah:
The God of Memphis.

Ptah-Hotep:
A vizier of the VI Dynasty, c. 2345–2181 BC.

Ra:
The sun God.

Sesostris:
A Pharaoh of the Middle Kingdom, c. 1971–1928 BC.

Sethi I:
A Pharaoh of the 19th Dynasty, 1301–1290 BC.

Stele:
A gravestone that usually identified the dead through name and titles.

Thoth:
Ibis-headed God of writing and knowledge.

The Two Lands:
Upper and lower Egypt.